Other Books by the Author

PoEmotions: Poems of Life, Love,
Faith, and All Emotions (2017)

PoEmotions Black History:
Our Origins, Our Struggles, Our Future (2018)

Flower Grow & Butterflies Fly and Other Short Poems (2019)

PoEmotions God & Faith (2020)

PoEmotions Black History: The Deeper the Roots (2021)

MY LIFE IN POEMS

. . . SO FAR

PATRICK L.C. MEADE

Thank you for your support.
Enjoy and be blessed!

Dedications

I would like to mention to these following people. You all have supported me and influenced me in one way or another. So, this is my return to you. For those that I don't mention, don't take it personally. Know that you are always in my heart and prayers. May God bless you all.

First and foremost, my Lord and Savior Jesus Christ
Thank you for blessing me with life and the talents that I have. Thank you for always forgiving me for my sins. I do not deserve any of Your glory, but You still love me. Without You, I would be nothing. So, I cannot thank You enough.

My Family
My mother and my father: The two people who brought me into God's great world. No more needs to be said about them.

My grandmother: My TV buddy growing up, who helped raise me into who I am today.

My godfather Elder Irvin L. George: The man who helped me and others form a closer relationship with Jesus Christ. Thank you for always keeping me and my family in your prayers. I know I will meet you again in Heaven someday.

Roy W. Harris II: My godbrother and one of the funniest

people that I have ever known. Thank you again and forever for blessing me with my godchild, Kendall Sophia Harris.

My Friends

Asia Sanders, Brittanie Dianne Croft and your mother Elizabeth Mills: You are a part of my extended family. You give me encouragement when I am at my lowest. I could never thank you three enough.

Tejon Witter, Justin Lyttleton, Christopher Lee & Derek Ntiomoah: My four brothers from other mothers. Thanks for sticking with me since high school.

To Lyn B. Mills-Nevills - Thank you for always believing in my dreams and for being such a great friend.

Contents

PART 3: THE LOVE I FEEL

PART 4: MEADISMS

PART 5: IN THE END . . .

My Life So Far & What Poetry Is to Me

I have had a pretty interesting life so far.

I was born on October 25, 1989, at Our Lady of Mercy Hospital in The Bronx, New York, at 12:42 p.m. My mom always made sure to give me the precise details of that day. I was my mom's little Butterball, a reference to the brand of turkey, because I was a big baby when I emerged from the womb. Though I was the only child my mother had, my childhood was basically normal. I still went to school Monday to Friday, did my homework, watched TV, played with my many toys and books, etc.

It wasn't until 2006 that my life started to get a little challenging.

Before my birthday, my mom was diagnosed with an illness, which was a real surprise to me. I was pretty concerned about how my mom would deal with this terrible disease, which she handled like nothing. It had an effect on my academics because I started to not perform to the best of my abilities at the start of my senior year in high school. However, this would not be the only challenge I would have in my senior year.

Around February 2007, I got a note from my father stating that he was locked up. It was an absolute shock for me. I knew that my dad had not been around during most of my childhood.

But to learn that it was because of what he told me, it really leveled me emotionally. There were times that I just wanted to scream out loud. Ultimately, I would persevere and still graduate with honors by the end of the school term.

In the midst of everything that was going on around me, I decided to experiment with poetry. I had read poetry before, being a lover of Maya Angelou especially. However, this would be the first time that I would try and do it on a regular basis. I've been doing poetry for nearly twenty years now. It's one of the best things that has come into my life, besides Jesus Christ. Usually, I'm not really good at expressing myself with other people. Writing words in stanzas helps me get my feelings out, even though no one is there in front of me.

All of the poetry that I have done so far is written from my heart. Sometimes, they are not the best poems in the world. But I still try to grow with it. I could create and write anything I want: about love, faith, the world that I see and hear around me. It's a great feeling to have. It helps me escape from all of the stresses that are in my life. Through poetry, I have finally been able to find my own voice. Although I have always a voice through singing in church and school talent shows, doing recitations and speeches in church (on top of singing and playing the organ & piano), poetry has given me a stronger way to express myself. I've passed out some of my material to my closest friends. To date, I have published five poetry books, one of them for children. Now, I am going to share this with you.

This book centers on some specific instances that have happened during my life so far that still resonate with me to this day. I wanted to take a different approach to the traditional autobiography and share my experiences and perspectives on things through poetry, as best I could. One day, I will publish a more traditional autobiography when I get to experience more of what God has laid out for me to see. However, I wanted to release this project in this format during this particular year for two reasons. First, it would coincide with me graduating with my master's degree in early childhood education from The City College of New York. The other is to help me celebrate my thirty-fifth birthday on October 25, which is a big milestone for me.

Though these are written from my perspective, some of the words may speak to you personally. Maybe you have dreams of love. Perhaps you fight with yourself every day about what you should do. You might even remember a time in your childhood. Maybe you just have something to say and you want to get it out of your system. For anyone who has the same desire that I had, and still have, this is for you too. If I can say anything to you, it would be this—have faith in yourself and God will take care of the rest.

I hope you enjoy what you read here.

PART 1

'89 AND RUNNIN'

My mom and her little Butterball

1989

Let me take you back to 1989
The start of this crazy life of mine
Right as I begin to say these rhymes
I remember things that have stood the test of time

George H.W. Bush walked in the White House
Ronald Reagan had already walked out
New year, new president, that's what it was about
'89 was the same year *Batman* came back out

Ted Bundy went to the electric chair
Soon later, Madonna was singing *"Like a Prayer"*
Then came protests at Tiananmen Square
Innocent people dying for rights that are fair

Rushdie released *The Satanic Verses*
To be met by Khomeini & a thousand curses
Rest in peace Lucille Ball, hello *Seinfeld*
The world's 1st Game Boy goes on sale

America tunes in to *The Simpsons*
While little kids play on their Sega Genesis
Then this...

October 25 at 12:42
My mom's 1st & only son came through
Patrick Laurence Charles Meade - that's me!!
Into the world, I now proceed

My 1st 365

My initial three hundred sixty-five
Were an interesting time to be alive

After 27 years, Mandela was finally free
In South Africa, apartheid finally ceased
Everyone could ride the same buses & same trains
Ending decades of segregation & the same games

Elsewhere, the Gulf War was about to start
But in America, you couldn't smoke in a bar

WalMart was first built
Chemical weapons plants were shut down
Germany finally said The Berlin Wall must come down

Ultimate Warrior beat Hulk Hogan clean
Became the new WWE king
Andre the Giant wrestled for the last time in a WWE ring

Nickelodeon & Universal Studios open
Where kids can be silly
While adults got stuck listening to Milli Vanilli
Okay, not really

The Simpsons ruled TV
But so did Big Willie
The Fresh Prince of Bel Air who came from South Philly

The Giants, Pistons & Reds sat on sports' thrones
While Macauly Colken sat *Home Alone*
Julia Roberts was a *Pretty Woman* & a stunning looker
Getting her start playing a stunning hooker

Doing the *Humpty Hump* was a thing on the rap scene
Tupac was doing it before he became a rap king
Biggie was still on the street, slinging to crack fiends
4 years before he became a rap king

Everyone got so angry over *Me So Horny*
Secretively, they must've begged their spouses
"Bone me!!"

Other things happened that I can't recall
Some parts were crazy
Other times, it was a ball

But soon, there would be much change
As I began to advance in age

By the Time I Was Five

---✦---

Mandela was President of South Africa
By the time I was five
Putting the final nail in the coffin of apartheid

But Rwanda was recovering from a genocide
Its people going through a great divide
Many corpses laid in the countryside

In America, Clinton was reelected President
Some people thought of him as a Heaven sent

By the time I was five, Nancy Kerrigan had cried
After she got clubbed from the blind side

By the time I was five, Biggie finally had arrived
Blowing up on the rap scene & igniting mics
From street hustler to rap superstar
No one thought that hip hop would go that far

But you can't forget about years before
Kicking down the door was Tupac Shakur
The product of the Panthers & a single mother
No other MC kept it real like this brother

He may have been labeled as a thug
But his mind was filled with wisdom & love
By the time I was five, OJ was accused of double homicide
After that white Bronco made that slow ride

Thanks to Cochran, O.J. gets found not guilty
White America felt that justice was filthy
Black America celebrated with pride
Into freedom, OJ would glide

By the time I was five, Kurt Cobain had committed suicide
Another bright young talent had died

A year after that, after I did turn five, Selena died
Murdered before her potential could be realized

Weeks before Selena died, Eazy-E got taken by AIDS
Before dying, he told the youth that AIDS is no game

Then, months after Eric Wright died
The media decided that two coasts had to collide
For years, the beef was low key
But on a good night, Suge Knight gave the media ammo to yell
"GO BEEF!"

Indirectly causing a great divide
Having everyone pick a side
Which do you rep?
East or West?

Bad Boy or Death Row?
No one would let go
Within a year and a half, 'Pac & Biggie would be dead so
The media would move on, saying "And...so?"

Michael Jackson had Lisa Marie for his wife
Was Elvis Presley's son in law for a brief time

The MLB had gone on strike
Owners and players would bargain and fight
John Bobbitt's penis got sliced off by a knife

Forrest Gump said a box of chocolate is what life is like
Mel Gibson was a *Braveheart* willing to fight
Will Smith & Martin Lawrence were some *Bad Boys*
Pixar made millions off a Story about glad Toys

Indeed, by the time I was five
It was an interesting time to be alive

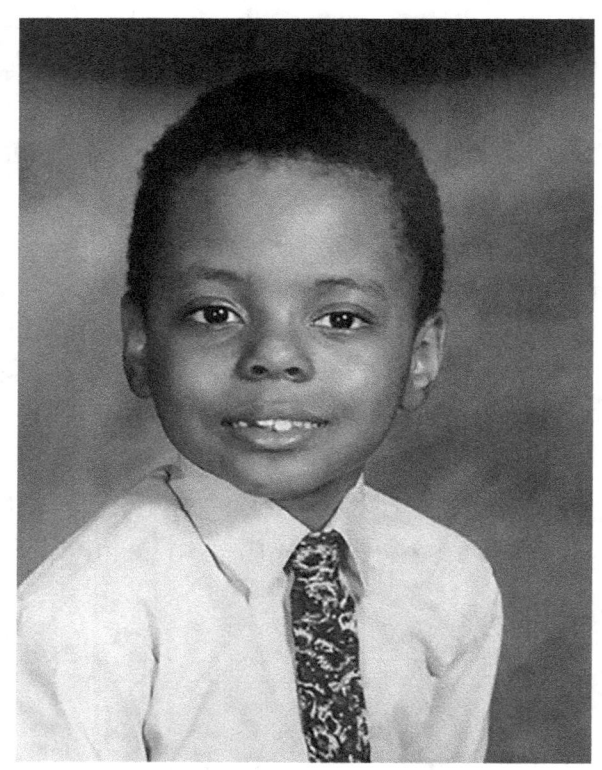

Mid 1990s

Runnin' through the 90s

After being beaten like a dog, Rodney King got no justice
While those 4 cops walk away
LA nearly blew up like the World Trade

Fires were burning long
Tensions were burning strong
Rodney said "Can we just get along?"

Farakkan gets thousands of black men to march
While Charles & Diana decide that they should part

Friends, Fraiser, Martin, 90210
Jaws dropped when Pam Anderson runs in slow mo

Women wanted their hair to look like Rachel
Men drooled when they saw Lara Croft on their console

Lady Di always beautiful in our eyes
When you left this Earth, we were all surprised
Seeing your funeral, I saw how much you were loved
You truly were England's rose, a peaceful dove

Even though you lived your life like a candle in the wind
Burning out too soon, but your legend never did
Rest in peace Mother Teresa, you're now a saint
Same to Jackie O, carried herself with such grace
JFK Jr. took his last flight
On one tragic night
The Kennedys lost its last shining light

Then we marveled at the strength of Lance Armstrong
MJ was in every commercial that was on
Foreman, 44, once again champion
But men still shook in fear at Mike Tyson

Clinton's still president
But he was busy having sex with Monica in his Office
He was impeached, but soon walked away
Then the world started worrying about Y2K

There was a bunch of hype
However, nothing happened at midnight
Everyone expected a catastrophe, but there was nothing
Media, think before you say something

So that's my 90s in a nutshell
If I forgot to mention anything, oh well

Cartoon Cartoons

Bugs Bunny was always sly and funny
Shaggy & Scooby were always high and hungry
Popeye taught me to eat spinach
So I can stay strong to the finish

While Yogi Bear scooped up picnic baskets
I learned to care for Earth from Captain Planet
Taught me not to be down with pollution
While Yosemite Sam was rootin', tootin' & shootin'

I was a super fan of the animated Superman
… and Batman
… and Spider-Man
… and any X-Man

Would watch Cartoon Network always
If I could, I'd be watching them all day

From Tom and Jerry reruns
To Road Runner speed runs
Speech therapy: Porky Pig & Elmer Fudd needed some

Dexter was a genius in the lab
Bad guys would get defeated with a jab
From Blossom, Bubbles or Buttercup
Pop 'em with no troubles with uppercuts

While Johnny Bravo tried to pick up chicks
And get told to kick up bricks
Cow & Chicken ate pork butts and taters
Ed, Edd & Eddy ate jawbreakers of many flavors

Ed was a dim wit, Double D was a genius
Eddy, always tried getting rich quick by scheming'
Samurai Jack swung swords at Aku the Demon
If Courage the Cowardly Dog saw one, he'd start screamin'

Though I enjoyed watching Teen Titans
The Justice League were some mean titans
An all-star team of an all-star dream
Out of this world like the MonStars team

That's a Space Jam reference
That was my favorite movie
True God
To this day, I'm still down with The Toon Squad

In this era of trends & newer slangs
I'm glad memories like these came back like Boomerang
Wow! I really shocked myself
I'm about to change the channel & watch myself

WrestleManiac (Part I)

Suplexes & bodyslams
Seeing bodies rammed
Into the canvas
Had me saying "Man, it's..."

The best thing that I've seen in the world
Like an Airplane Spin almost making a man hurl
Larger than life figures on my TV screen
Were so fast & strong that you would hear me scream

In excitement & joy
It was amazing for this little boy

Randy Savage dropping elbows from the sky
Yokozuna crashing down with the Banzai!!!
Hulk Hogan dropping his leg
Bret Hart making pretzel knots out of legs

Undertaker taking souls to Tombstone City
Shawn Michaels superkicking people down, looking so pretty
Scott Hall send foes off the Razor's Edge
Bam Bam Bigelow scorched with his blazing head
The late 90s were the best of times

In which I was blessed to find
A war was going on through TV screens
For fans like me, it was a sweet dream

Monday Nights were the bomb
With *Nitro & RAW*
The remote control never left my palm

One minute, I'd see Sting fight the n.W.o
The next, I'd check out The Rock & Stone Cold
Later on, watch Goldberg spear people down like "Fuck it!!"
Next minute, hear DX tell some fool "Suck it!!"

The Nitro Girls did appease me
The Godfather showed that pimpin' ain't easy
Women screamed for Val Venis
And dreamed to see Val's penis

Cruiserweights were high flyers like planes
Heavyweights couldn't set fires like Kane
Unless it was his big brother, The Undertaker
Monstrous & demonic soul breakers

Seeing Mick Foley thrown off the Hell in a Cell
Get up & still have a story to tell
Seeing Sable show off her breasts
While Chyna threw clotheslines at men's chests

After bugging out over Y2K
Everyone was bugging out over Y2J
Everyone had saw or had to hear it, yo!

Every Monday night became RAW Is Jericho

Edge & Christian, Hardys & Dudleys
Had TLC matches that were beautifully ugly
High stakes for high reward
For all they did, I hold them in high regard

The Attitude Era was an absolute pleasure
The Attitude Era was an absolute treasure
For fans like me
No as a man, I see

It really was the best of times

Dead Man's Tale

Taking souls and digging holes
I was a fan before I turned 6 years old
Specifically, I've loved him since I was three
He had powers to make men flee

Figuratively, he put tags on toes
Rolling them in caskets & letting the lid close
Cold solitude making their skin cold

No matter what men did to him
He would get up
Like Lazarus from the crypt
He would sit up

No matter if they were giants or monsters
Deranged or bizarre
He would cut them down with ease like trees
He was my favorite by far

Whether he wore gold or not
I was sold a lot
So to you, I give all the props

To the original Dead Man
The Man from the Dark Side
The Phenom

The American Bad Ass
Big Evil

They'll be no others like him
Even if there are 6 sequels

To The Last Outlaw, be blessed with peace
Your legend will never...
Rest...in...peace

Runnin' thru the New Millenium

The Feds came to pick up Elian
Meanwhile we had to deal with a crazy election
Instead of Al Gore walking on the White House lawn
George Walker Bush won

Then came 9/11, when I was still eleven
1 month away from twelve when the Twin Towers fell
So after this, we began to move fast
In Afghanistan looking for bin Laden's ass

But just when the troops were on the right track
About face, march to Iraq
They said Saddam had weapons of mass destruction
One lie in one great construction
When we got there, what'd we find?
Nothing!!!

So why the hell did we go there for?
Can you answer my question, Michael Moore?

Sierra Leone, people dying over diamonds

While everybody else is worrying about the climate
Katrina hit, thousands are dying
You didn't do enough FEMA, stop lying
Those displaced start crying
Rebuilding their lives, they're trying

Okay, let's take a look at some pop culture

On YouTube, you could see my video
But was my face on MySpace? No!!
Okay, please strike a pose
I want to take a picture of you on my iPhone

Then came the Crackberry
I mean the Blackberry
Shout out to Denzel Washington & Halle Berry

Big up to Mo'nique, Jamie Foxx & Forrest Whitaker
Taking home the Oscar
Continue to prosper

I'm drunk off reality shows
My brain's starting to swell, I think I've overdosed

I'm tired of it now, I can take no more
I may be get screwed more than the cast of *Jersey Shore*
That includes Snooki
I admit I kind of like you

But you took me to the brink of insanity
It was so bad, I thought I'd get a nose bleed

At least it wasn't Bieber Fever
I'd rather get knocked out with ether

So, before I throw up
Let me find out which couple broke up
But I won't get choked up
I'll just grow up
Hold up

Everybody wants a video of stars having sex
Some of them are grainy and none are the best
This part of my poem, I'd like to forget
So, let's just move on to see what's next

WrestleManiac (Part II)

By 2001, the competition would lessen
When WCW got bought, fans like me got the impression
That some big names would come to the big stage
Wrestling would be fun in a lot of big ways

Though I was hoping a lot
I was hoping for naught
Dream matches on a grand scale were forgot

No Hogan, Hall or Nash
To make all the cash
No Savage, Sting or Goldberg
Oh, I was so hurt

But forward the business kept pressin'
Into an era of Ruthless Aggression
Kurt Angle & Eddie Guerrero got more space to shine
Some new faces stepped into prime time

Brock Lesnar
John Cena
Batista & Randy Orton
Ran with newly lit torches

While Triple H ruled with Evolution
TNA was having its own revolution
AJ Styles defied gravity with aerial insanity
Samoa Joe would smoke people out
When he choked people out

2010: Hogan & Bischoff tried recreating the Monday Night War
They really shouldn't have
Recapture magic from the 90s
They really couldn't have

In WWE, it became quite calm
'Til in 2011, a Chicago Made Punk dropped a pipe bomb
Letting off steam from his mind
During the summer, it would come alive

Thinking things in the 'E' would become cool again
But Vinny Mac said "Things needed to be cooled my friends"
Can't run the risk & have others run the ship
Some things must remain the same

C'mon Vince!!!

Daniel Bryan make folk believe by making them say "YES!!!"
No one could conceive that it would be a success
Leading to a Miracle on Bourbon Street
On the same night Brock Lesnar broke The Streak

Damn!!!
Though time has passed, oft I still scorn
It shattered my heart & chilled warmth

For more than a little while
But The Dead Man is still my hero
Though I'm not a little child

Though things in the 'E' are far from perfect
There are still stars going hard
Stardom, they deserve it

Finally, at long last, McMahon chose
To look to the indy scene
Scoop up Seth Rollins & Dean Ambrose

Along with Finn Balor, Sami Zayn & Kevin Owens
Those dudes stand close
Shining bright like a mega watt lamppost

Then, they got Joe, Nakamura & AJ Styles
Making the inner fanboy in me smile
Though they push Roman Reigns to growing pains
Rivers in WWE don't flow the same

Finally, lest I forget
Some talented ladies are finally getting legit respect
Though Chyna, Lita & Trish had caught fire like Katniss
They only got 5 minutes for a match
What happened?

Instead of matches & stories to a make a packed room shake
For years, women's segments were time for a bathroom break
Did Vince ignore them & just not care?
Would he if his daughter had been dropped there?

Whether it was Mickie James, Victoria, Melina or Torrie
They only got a few minutes to have glory
Then Charlotte, Sasha Banks, Becky Lynch, Bayley and the like
Showed that women deserve that big spotlight

Like DDP would say, "That's not a bad thing
That is a good thing
Seeing all that in a 20 X 20 foot ring

I can never lie
Though one day, I'll have a wife
Wrestling is my mistress
My love for it will never die

Singin'

By fifth grade, something started to come alive
It was after I listened to *Mambo Number 5*
The words and beat were so catchy
The urge to sing would suddenly catch me

Though I would come to learn it was about sex
I couldn't expect what would come about next
With talent growth, I'd hit up school talent shows
Then it would glide through all the way to high school

But most of all, I got to sing in church
Most often, I was the loudest voice to be heard
Soon, my talent would take me higher
From the Joy Bells to the Senior Choir

But then in college, I started writing my own verses
Most are clean, but a few have curses
But it's my way of expressing myself
Whenever I sing or rap, I bless someone else

So, just like a famous Andrea Crouch song
I'm Gonna Keep on Singin' strong

PART 2

COMING OF AGE

When the Towers Fell

When the Towers fell
Getting coverage on the news
I was still in school
Starting to get confused

Children kept getting called to go home
In my mind, I'm thinking "What's going on?"
Was there an emergency?
Causing everyone to leave urgently?

Soon that afternoon, the children were called to the church
Like the rest of the world, we learned the worst
Something bad happened downtown &
I feared for my mom's safety
Praying that she would come home safely

When Grandma brought me home, I learned what was wrong
I also learned that hate was something that was strong
A force of evil caused The Twin Towers to fall
Innocent lives taken in it all

Though my mom made it home late
The important thing was that she made it home safe
Though evil caused The Towers to fall
It caused America to stand tall

We wouldn't let ourselves be shaken by hate
We would stand firm & be great

Junior Year, St. Raymond High School for Boys
Forever a Raven!!

Dysfunctionality

I always knew I had a mother
But I didn't see my father
"Ask why?" sometimes I want to
But I mostly didn't bother

I just thought this is how God meant it to be
But to me, it was still a big mystery
As I grew older and the world got colder
I had to learn to bear everything on my shoulders

2006, a month before I turned 17
My mother got sick and I got stressed
I was on the road to college, this year should've been my best
All I could do was ask the Lord, "What's next?"

But then I turned seventeen
I heard about the tragedy
That do this day still affects me

A note from my dad like any other day
When I read what he had to say
I thought the sky was turning grey

I started losing faith, didn't see a way
That God could ever make a change
But my mom is healed, my dad's keeping it real
Nothing could ever explain the joy I feel

Although I've borne this pain for so long
I just have to stand strong & learn to carry on
With God on my side, I'll be able to hang on
He'll guide me to the right & keep me from the wrong

Now I don't know if anyone is just like me
And lived a life full of dysfunctionality
You could make it through, it's real easy
Let go, let God & just believe

Dream Lover

It's like a bad love song
I fall for the prettiest woman I see

A girl with a nice complexion
Easily the object of my affection
It's hard for me to keep my attention

But she's a woman that I probably can't have
It doesn't stop me from trying though

I've got to find her
I've got to find her
I won't stop until I make her my girl

But for now, she's just a dream
I just have to imagine how things could be

Imagine if we got married
If we ever have kids
Oh well, I could still dream

Friend of Mine

Dedicated to Asia Sanders

Even though I know you well
The way I really feel about you, I was so scared to tell
My worst fear was that you would say "Go to Hell"
But in time, you helped me break down out my shell

I know I told you that my life's been hard
But you said "It's okay. Just leave it to God"

Because He supplies everything that you need
Walking with you, guiding you through struggles unseen
But when I looked into your eyes, I saw the Sun beam
Listening as I shared with you my dreams

I know this must be a blessing from Heaven above
Having a friend like you, that's real love
Even though I have to sit & watch time fly
I know that you'll always be a true friend of mine

Crazy Little Sister

Dedicated to Brittanie Sanders

Sometimes I just can't figure her out
Sometimes she makes me want to shout
Even though she has a million-dollar smile
This girl is sometimes wild

Sometimes I just can't figure her out
Especially 'cause of what comes out of her mouth
I don't know what she's going to do or say
I wonder if I should move closer or stay away

But for some reason, I still love her the same
So, I really can't complain
That's my little sister, another dear friend of mine
Let our friendship last for all time

Slippin'

Grandma's losing her memory
She barely remembers me
Don't know how long this will be

Asking the same questions
After the answers are mentioned
Her mind's in another dimension
Walking around aimlessly with no direction

Wondering in a haze for the rest of her days
With her body racked in pain
Memories keep fading away

She doesn't recognize certain faces
Not even where a certain place is
Doesn't know the month or the day
Not much I could or say

Imagination has become reality
Now lost in insanity
When you tell her she's wrong
She says she's right

She's just slippin'
Can't outrun the hands of time
Things are no longer sublime
She's just slippin'

She can't recognize old from new
But there's nothing much I can do
As she slips away

Not knowing who she is anymore
Not knowing what she's doing anymore
She doesn't know what's going on
Unaware of right & wrong

Skies get greyer every day
It keeps on getting darker
She can't see anything anymore

Running (From Who?)

I'm running down the street as far as I can
Bystanders confuse me for a marathon man
Wondering who I'm running from
But I'm thinking straight & all I can do is run

The one I'm running from could be a dangerous man
Because he knows he has the world in the palm of his hand
Inside his mind are dreams and schemes
Of making some green on the world's scene

Sometimes he shakes me with fear
Getting so shook, I nearly burst into tears
He's always changing lanes
So much it drives another man insane

You're probably wondering who this could be
Well, that man is me

Wrestling with Myself

Step into the ring, the crowd begins to scream
They come to see me go & do my thing
I've done my warmups
I've shown up

I'm ready to rumble, I have no time to fumble
But my heart starts to crumble
When I look up the aisle & see
That the opponent that I'm facing here tonight is me

He walks the same way that I do
Talks the same way that I do
In fact he looks like me
I can't take him lightly

Because I know he came to fight me
I look him in the face
My heart starts to race
When he says "I'm going to take you out & take your place"

Even though I'm speaking figuratively
Wrestling with myself is what I do literally
Every day I pray that I'll be able to find a way
To win the fight of my life & stand in God's light

Because the other side of me is lost in greed
More concerned with what he wants more than what he needs
As I proceed, let me just say
That everybody else goes through this every single day

Whether your soul is locked in a steel cage
With all the rage that your body can sustain
You need to take the pain

Because you'll get thrown to the wall like a basketball
People may start to count you out when you fall
With blood in your eyes, but you still rise
When your bad self tells you to lay down & die

But I can't cry, just keep fighting on
Put my trust in the Lord & stand strong
Although my body is sore & it begins to shake
Dear God, don't let my spirit break

Victory let me take from the depths of defeat
Let Satan fall on his face at my feet
Let me turn the tables because I know God is able
To deliver me for His love is unbreakable

For Satan, the Holy Spirit is unbearable
He's so terrible 'cause he's scared of me & you

Walk out the cage victorious
For the God that I serve is so glorious

My weary soul is restored back to health
I've won after wrestling with myself

If I Could Just Run Away

If I could just run away
I would run away today
I wouldn't even hesitate
I would run with no delay

Because the life I'm living isn't going that well
Sometimes, I feel like I'm living in Hell
Every day, I'm oppressed by stress
Lord, deliver me from all of this mess

Sometimes, things for me get too tough
Sometimes, things for me get too rough
Making me want to scream because I've had enough
Everything around me is sometimes too much

If I could run away, I may end up changing my mind
If I ran away, I would just be running blind
So, I have to stay strong each and every day
Though sometimes, I still consider running away

Me & My Pen

Me & my pen are like 2 best friends
We may fall off for a minute, but get together again
My pen writes the poetry that comes from the flow in me
Sometimes I have to let go & let God take control of me

As I lay my ink on the page
Dreaming of a day when I can hear my words of a stage
If not, then I'm just happy that I found a voice
Nothing forced on me, all my choice

To let myself be heard through the words that I speak
With the power that I could reach each with clear speech

The Fame

The fame is very strange
Everyone seeks it
The money, the prestige & recognition

The fame has its benefits
Mansions, famous friends, etc.
But like most things in life, there's a dark side

We've all seen it
The excess, the drugs and other problems
Everyone wants a piece of you
Temptation surrounds you at every turn

So many talented people have been swallowed
up by the dark side of fame
Hendrix, Joplin, Morrison
Their genius was manifest
But their demons took over

Even today we see it
Michael, Amy, Whitney, Prince and others
The evilness of drugs took over their lives
The evilness stole their lives

I still dream about what it would be to be rich & famous
But I often question whether it would be worth it
Would I want to deal with all the extra stress and problems?
The paparazzi
The tabloids and gossip

People pandering to me (for good or bad)
Would it be worth it all?

Dormant (I've Got a Story to Tell II)

Based on a poem from my 1st book, *PoEmotions:
Poems of life, love, faith and all emotions*

I've worked in silence in the midst of violence
Moving to find treasure like a pirate
Putting up with trials & tribulations
Trying to resist temptations

In the hopes of becoming a better man
In the hopes that I could take a better stand
In my own life to do what's right
One day, I hope to make my dream girl my wife

But I've learned that to get to Heaven
You got to go through Hell
But I've made it through
I've got a story to tell

I want to be known for my paragraphs
Something significant to write on my epitaph
Leaving a legacy a legacy for others to follow
Knowing that they can make a new tomorrow

It's more valuable than any worldly possession
Being able to move through life with progression
Learning every lesson while trying to ease stresses
Like a man pushing a boulder uphill, he still presses

That's the same thing with me
'Cause God's in control & I believe
Now I know I could break from my shell
Like an inmate from his cell

Now I've got a story to tell

Let Me Be

Everyone pulls me every which way
Saying that I should walk this way
Talk this way
Like everyone else

Instead of letting me be myself, I have to be politically correct
Keeping my true feelings in check
I can't give thanks to my God for all He's done
For bringing me from where I started from

They should just let me be

Don't let me be restricted or conflicted
God has blessed me & I'm spiritually gifted
My words are spoken to get you lifted
Because when you feel this, you feel the realness

Giving God thanks for blessing me
With a right mind and letting me be free

In a world full of constant change
He has kept me sane & kept me the same
It feels so good to be free
It feels so good to let me be me

Looking for a Rainbow

Like Dorothy Gale on her way to Oz
So many like me pray to God
Asking for a ray of light
Hoping it will be bright

So many like me are looking for a rainbow
Every time their pain grows
Too many clouds have come abound
Frustrations start to mount

Causing tears to fall from our eyes
Like raindrops from the skies
The sky growing cool
In the midst of the dew

We can't stop looking for a rainbow
We can't let our heads hang low
It's somewhere out there
So, never be afraid to dare

30 Y.O.

Written to celebrate my 30th birthday in 2019

I can't believe it!!
Making it to 30 years on Earth is quite an achievement
It's hard to think how far I've come
It's hard to think how far I've run

I've seen 5 Presidents & experienced their precedents
Including one who thought he was a Heaven sent
I was raised on gospel music, wrestling & cartoons
Some of my memories are still sharp as harpoons

From Bugs Bunny chomping on carrots saying *What's up Doc?*
To Scooby & Shaggy's hunger pains that were nonstop
Because they were high
Watching Batman, Spider Man & X-Men
showed me superheroes were fly

Cartoon Network was the bomb spot
I could binge watch nonstop
Then flip to MTV to watch rap, rock, pop
I may have had my 1st hard on watching Lady Marmalade
With Christina, Lil Kim, Pink & Mya – My God

Whenever I saw Janet, I could say, "Dammit!"
She looks so fine like a bottle of wine

The 3 Children of Destiny always took the breath of me
Or was it four of them
I know there was more of them
It was like there was a revolving door of them

Before I plunge my mind in hedonistic sin
Let me remind myself what God did within
He guided me to Kirk Franklin, who taught me to *Stomp*
On the Devil's head till he ran back to Hell's swamp

God brought me back to church where I grew my voice
That I found in a 5th grade talent show
But, He had instilled the will for me to grow
Learned to play the piano & organ
Now, my Sunday mornings are never boring

I lift my voice when I sing
Always to my Savior & King
Without Him, I am nothing
With Him, I can do all things

My love for wrestling I will never outgrow
Pride for my 1st love, I will always show
Much love to The Undertaker, Stone Cold & The Rock
The nWo were 2 Sweet to watch
Much love to my modern-day faves that grace my airwaves
Like John Cena, Sasha Banks, Bray Wyatt & Roman Reigns

Now, my greatest love is the pen
One of my closest & dearest friends
Helping me express myself in the best ways
Bringing ease to where stress lays

Now, I am blessed to share my words with you
Experiencing firsthand what the power of words will do

I still have more dreams to achieve
More things to make a reality
Put out some books & make some million dollars back
Find a pretty woman to holler at

God has let me see 30 years old
I am ready to see 30 years more
He's not through with me yet
So, forward I step

Under Siege

My response to the Capital riot on January 6, 2021

Never in my wildest dreams
Did I ever envision one of the wildest scenes
One of America's symbols put under siege
With broken glass & violent screams

All because one man couldn't take a loss
America's reputation paid a cost
It's such a terrible shame
In all of this, who do we blame?

We can blame the cult that caused the revolt
Their corrupted devotion created so much erosion
An erosion of common sense & logic
Acting violently because of one man's nonsense

We can blame politicians for being enablers
When they should have been disablers
Instead, they got blinded by the scheme
Thinking it was cool because he was on their team

They kept giving him a false sense of power
Every day & every hour
Common sense was devoured
Those that didn't stand for right were cowards

Of course, we should blame the messenger
We should blame the deceiver as much
as his enablers & believers

His toxic rhetoric caused the siege
See worldwide on screens
His toxic rhetoric caused the rage
That burst onto the Capital uncaged

This was the consequence of power unchecked
This was democracy's greatest threat
This never should have gone so far
This set a terribly low bar

Now after the siege, we have to learn
Otherwise, society will once again burn
If we fail to learn, history will be repeated
Let's be smart & let ignorance be defeated

If My Blackness Scares You

If my blackness scares you, don't be alarmed
My blackness isn't a sign you'll be harmed
My blackness is just who I am
It's one of my traits as a man

If my blackness scares you, please check yourself
That paranoia is bad for your health
You fear what you may not understand
Thinking my blackness should be damned

My blackness isn't a cause for fright
My blackness is a beautiful sight
It shines in the brightest days
It illuminates in the darkest nights

My blackness should never be slighted
My blackness should never be blocked
Though it sometimes gets mocked
My blackness will never be stopped

So, if my blackness scares you, it's not my fault
It's too precious to be kept in a vault
My blackness needs to be free
My blackness needs to be seen

My blackness is amazing and true
If my blackness scares you, well...

BOO!!!

Coming Home

Dedicated to my father

It was a day I had waited on for years
When it happened, I didn't know if I would burst into tears
It happened when I was at the movies
When I got the news that would move me

My dad had finally come home!

My heart was filled with surprise
A sparkle of joy may have filled my eyes
This indeed was a dream come true
A new sense of hope began to run through

Eventually, we can finally meet each other
Exchange pleasantries as we greet each other
Trying to catch up on all the time that passed
To form a stronger bond that lasts

We are no longer separated by bars
I couldn't wait for the day we held each other in our arms
All I can say is thank you to God and God alone
My father is finally home!!!

More Pictures and Memories

Young me riding in style

Walking in style early on

High school graduation with Tejon Witter, Justin
Lyttleton, Christopher Lee & Derek Ntiomoah

My last trip in Atlantic City
Can't wait to go back there one day!

College Graduation from The City College of New York, 2012

The crew – Adriana Zarzuela, Christopher Lee, Derek
Ntiomoa, Justin Lyttleton and Tunisia Mitchell

Taken after Justin graduated college

InspiredWordNYC.com

Performing spoken word poetry, 2018

Much love and respect to Mike Geffner, Marvin Mendlinger
and Inspired Word NYC for allowing me the opportunity
to express myself through spoken word poetry.

I promise you that one day, I will come back and perform on your stage.

Me with one of my best friends forever, Brittanie
Sanders, when I celebrated my 33rd birthday

Reuniting with my dad after many years!

PART 3

THE LOVE I FEEL

Beautiful Woman

Every time I see your face
I see a symbol of God's grace
You bring peace & joy to my soul
You're a blessing in this world

You're as beautiful as Marilyn Monroe
You would be good to love, kiss & hold
You have the grace of Lady Di
I see it when I look in your eyes

Your beauty could just stop time
How I wish you could be mine
But I am happy to call you friend
I hope this feeling never ends

Because I could no longer pretend
I know you're always there for me
You are a true friend indeed
I know you feel the same for me

Tongue Tied

It may sound cliché
But finding words to say to a woman is never easy
So, I struggle

A million thoughts run through my head
My greatest dread is that the wrong
words could get me in trouble
And then I crumble

'Cause I may never get to see her again
Which would be akin to never ever breathing again

We may be friends
But we can be more
My knuckles bleed from constantly knocking on steel doors

The answer is that "I love you" if you ever ask why
But I could never say it with pride

When I find the strength to say it
I get suffocated
By my own fears
The prettiest woman that I've known for years

May walk away & never come back
When I call in vain, she'll never run back

Out of sight, out of reach
Unable to shout or speak
To turn her around
Love's lost, never to rebound

But I still prey that one day
All of love's games we can play
Then I could say with pride
I love you, without getting tongue tied

Someone Else

I have my eyes on this girl
Priceless like diamonds & pearls
She looks so fine
I really want to make her mine

I tell her about the way I feel
And the way I feel is real
But then inside I go beside myself
When she tells me she's in love with someone else

Even in the midst of this, I still love her
It may take her longer to discover
That I want to be loved by her
And nobody else but her

Once I was shy by choice
But now thanks to you, I've found my voice
We should never be enemies
'Cause you're such a good friend to me

I'm hoping that we could be more
So open your heart & let love open the door
Maybe a deeper love will form in time
And by God's grace, we'll be entwined

But for now, I'm still sitting by myself
While she sits with someone else

You Are Love

You may never know how I truly feel
But through you I got a taste of something real
You gave me a song
Giving me the faith to stand strong

I don't know what the future holds
Where the road ends
Whether we'll become lovers or remain just friends

But I still give thanks to the Lord above
And I give thanks to you
Because you are love

Mystique

Roses may be red & violets may be blue
But the color of your heart is always so true
There is no better one than you
Join with me and one could be two

I want to include you in everything
Because to my world, more joy you bring
I believe we were meant to be together to never sever
Walking side by side no matter the weather

You're a true wonder of the world
I wonder how God could create such a beautiful girl
With the perfect brain & the perfect shape
I need to make my move, I can't hesitate

When I look inside your eyes, it's hard
for me to even concentrate
Even though we've gone around town before
It always feels like our first date
You're a sight I've never seen before

You're so unique
There's something about you that I adore
It's your mystique

I Don't Want a Beyonce

---✞---

I don't want a Beyonce to be my lady
I don't need a diva to be my queen of Sheba
She doesn't always have to rock diamonds on her neck
I'll love her no less & still give her respect

She doesn't have to be a Katy Perry or Mariah Carey
Dear God, that would be too scary
'Cause believe me, I'll lock my door
If she turns out to be a media whore

I don't want any of the Kardashians
How about Lindsay Lohan?
Hell no man!

If a girl likes to be in a scandal
That would be too much drama for me to handle
Burning dry like wax on a candle

She doesn't have to be shaped like an hour glass
Pretty face, small waist, nice ass...
Okay, I'm lying

But all that matters to me is the love that she'll be supplying
Keep me happy & pleased so I won't be crying
So again, I'll say
I don't want a Beyonce

What I'd Like . . .

You could be the girl next door
I won't love you less, only more
You could be an intellectual miss
I'll never diss, just long to kiss your lips

You could be humble & modest
I'll still worship you, my goddess
As long as you stay honest
I'll shower you with respect

You don't always have to lick your lips or shake your hips
With me, you'll never find a more real love than this
You don't have to strike a pose or shed your clothes
You're as swift as the wind that blows

You don't have to flirt to turn me on
No matter what you wear, you got it going on
You don't need to be a video girl to win my love
You don't have to be a video girl to be the one that I dream of

You can just be yourself
And all will be well

When I Say, "I Love You"

When I say I love you, I don't say it as a formality
It's not said because it's popular
I say it because I mean it
I say because there's a special place in my heart for you
You may not realize it
But you are a gift God has given me

So, I cherish you

You are my friend
My sister
A shoulder I could lean on
A kind soul

I love you

I Know You've Been Watching

Dedicated to my friend Lyn Mills

I know you've been watching me
You've watched me work and strive
You've watched me struggle and fall
Through it all, I have never quit

You've seen my joy
You've seen my anger
You've seen my moments of uncertainty
& helped me get clarity
You know of my works of charity

Even though you say I should slow down
I still try to push myself so far that I almost collapse
So far that my body gives in when my heart doesn't want to
But that's how far I will go

My challenges may be tough
But I am tougher

Making Up (For Lost Time)

Twenty-five years and Lord knows how many days
Is a mighty long time for things to change
That was how long I hadn't seen my father
Admittedly, there were times that my heart was bothered

I wished that he had seen all of my special moments
Talent shows and graduations – sharing happy emotions
Though we sent messages to each other from far away
Now and again, my mind still felt the strain

But now, that's all in the past
Now, we have a chance to make moments that last
We have already begun taking the first steps
Going out eating, movies and texts

We have more memories and a lot of time
To do anything that comes to mind
This is something that I look forward to
Making up for lost time together with you

Love you, Dad

Dear Godfather II

Dedicated to my godfather Elder Irvin Lyrell George
A follow-up to the poem *Dear Godfather* from
my book *PoEmotions: God and Faith*

Dear Godfather
It's been over 5 years since you went away
I think about you each and every day
Even though it was your time to go
Honestly, I still miss you so

I miss talking to you for a while after church service
Your words always giving me advice and purpose
You helped me keep my mind at ease
Because in God, there is perfect peace

You taught me the importance of living ready
You taught me to always keep my ship steady
Even though the winds and waves will shake me still
They always have to obey God's holy will

When I last saw you, you still had fight
Wanting to rise up with all of your might
I prayed that you'd be alright
Ultimately, God knew what was right

When He finally called you home, I knew you were pleased
All of your aches and pains finally ceased
Finally, you could rest
You ran your race and passed your tests

If you had a chance to come back, you would decline
Where you are now, you're just fine
So, my mind has made amends
One day, I know I'll see you again

When I do, we'll walk those streets of gold
We won't worry about growing old
What joyous day it will be
Together again – you and me

Forevermore, I will love you so
'Til we meet again, onward we go

Thank You

Dedicated to my mother and grandmother

There's no way I can pay you back
But the plan is to show you that I understand
You are appreciated

Tupac Shakur (*Dear Mama*)

Thank you mom for giving me life
Thank you mom for raising me right
Though it wasn't easy, you did more than your best
Forever, you are loved and blessed

Words cannot express how much you have done
Truly, I am one grateful son
Though at times, we may disagree
You still mean so much to me

Thank you grandma for nurturing me
Spending our days off together was a pleasure for me
Watching talk shows and soap operas
Was absolutely awesome

You were my tag team partner watching wrestling
Looking back at it, it was the best thing
Though your memory faded, its sight
brought a gleam to your eye
Something that I wish to see one more time

To both of you, my guardians and friends
I love you both with no end

PART 4

MEADISMS

See My Vision

———————✦———————

Walking through the world blind with eyes wide open
While in reality, some doors are closing
Love & peace replaced by anger and greed
Close your eyes for a moment while I tell you what you need

You don't need a reason to hide your religion
Take a few more moments so you could see my vision
No worries and no stress
Just somewhere with happiness

You could be yourself
Pressure from no one else

You don't need the criticism and the drama
All who could judge you is God & your mama
No politics from hypocrites
No one can take the joy you're coming with

Not the Devil or the President
Because there's a God you're not ashamed to represent

Legendary

Want to be known for much bigger things in life
Don't want to stay in the darkness
Longing for light

Want to do something bigger
Expand yourself quicker
Realizing you could be part of a much bigger picture

Got the motivation, got the dedication
To be front & center like the United Nations

Fears are holding back the greatest minds that there could be
Ignorance from others blocks the
greatness that they should see

Some may give up, never to live up
To the potential they could have
The reality's sad

But there are still those who shun the criticism
Seeing it as nothing but mindless cynicism

So they keep progressing with every word and sentence
So they could stand on the mountaintop,
screaming "I am legend"

Continue to keep your heads up & learn your lessons
Your greatest weapon is progression
Taking down obstacles some see as impossible
Those that state their doubts really don't have a clue
About the future legend that exists in you

Whether you're gifted with the pen or the voice
The bottom line is that you're gifted & you've got a choice

On how you want to expand your horizons
Even in ways that might seem surprising

For those that don't know your hustle, your flow
Like a seed from concrete, you continue to grow

Into something seemingly sent from Heaven
And the world beholds a new legend

Not Enough Love

Love is a word that comes and goes
But no one seems to really know
What it is to love anymore

We think it's just a one night stand
Not bothering to hold hands
What are we looking for?

Some lovers don't ask for each other's name
Just care about increasing their game
Something to talk about to their friends
Next night, they'll do it again

We find time to love material things
Whatever it is
But we all need to discover
The most important thing we need to love is each other

Fathers and mothers, sisters and brothers
Even those distant lovers
Love conquers hate
We need to let it rule before it's too late

Because there's not enough love today
Can't let something so precious slip away

We need that true love
We need that wonderful love
We need that everlasting love
There's not enough love

Sometimes I'd Rather . . .

Sometimes I'd rather be an ordinary
guy than a Hollywood celebrity
'Cause today, the meaning of fame isn't what it used to be
Most definitely, I'd rather stay true to my essence
Sometimes I'd rather relive my adolescence

Sometimes I'd rather be fat & out of shape
Eating collard greens & neckbones
Than look like a supermodel
Looking like skin & bones

Sometimes I'd rather be poor than rich
'Cause I'm afraid I'd turn into an egotistical bitch
But in the same breath, I'd rather be rich than poor
So my mom won't have to work anymore

I'd rather be a teacher & educate the youth
Than to be a politician who distorts the truth
Sometimes I'd rather be a preacher who tries to save souls
Than to be a stock broker who only counts bank rolls

I'd rather be married & bored than single & lonely
I'm longing for the day where a woman can hold me
When that happens, I'd rather have her be a plain Jane
Than a diva who always gossips & sprays names

But there's something more important that I should tell
I'd rather live eternity in Heaven than suffer forever in Hell

Gotham City

America is like the streets of Gotham
Many people have plots
How do you stop them?

Many are lost in schemes and corruption
Blurring lines between truth and obstruction

So many Jokers, Riddlers and Two Faces
Either insane, playing mind games
Or refusing to stay on a true basis

Everyone is in it for their own goals
Scarecrows prey on fear for your own souls

Just to bring pain to sobriety
Turning into the Bane of society

Dressed dapper like a Penguin, suit and tie
Trying to bring anguish to you and I

Veins filled with Poison Ivy
Trying to make us like Harley Quinn, loving blindly

The leaders who say they love us
But all they do is misuse and abuse us

Everyone wants to gain victory
But their hearts turn cold like Mr. Freeze

Some have clay faces that keep changing form
Always rearranging norms

America's full of minds who go strange
Then try to hit dead shots to your brain

Bringing death strokes to those that step
In the wrong path as Jokers let out strong laughs

The Demon's Head wants to erase those
Who interfere with his perfect plan
Of his visions of a perfect land

Courts of Owls watching and planning
When they're ready to strike, they'll send out their Talons

To go and do their bidding
Doesn't matter if they're sinning
As long as they're winning

Other characters may lurking under the surface
Creating schemes to serve their own purpose

We to up the anti & be vigilant
Even if it means being militant
But do it responsibly while we still live
These days, it's so easy for good people to become villains

H.U.G.

A hug is a great sign of love
One of God's gifts from above

A hug says "I love you"
A hug says "What's good?"
A hug can lift you from the ground where you stood

A hug is a sweet caress
A hug can help ease pain and stress
A hug can comfort someone who's lonely
Or tell someone you love they're your one & only

But if you look beyond the surface & explore
The letters H,U,G, can mean much more

H.U.G. can mean Happy Under God
For He gets you through times that hare hard
Or it could mean I'm a Human Understanding Grace
That I see when I look at your face

So, when I say I'm a hugger
You can say I'm a Human Understanding
God's Grace is Ever Reaching
Daily trying to learn His teachings
Or that I'm Happy & Unshaken Given Great Eternal Resolve

So, don't be ashamed to hug
You're only spreading God's love

It's a Woman's World
(Men Just Live in It, Sometimes)

I'm not trying to sound soft
I'm just calling it as I see it
Anything a man can be in the world
A woman can also be it

From an architect to a billionaire exec
But if you cross her the wrong way
She'll reach for your neck

Whether it's your mother or your girlfriend
Women are the real deal
They don't pretend

Besides God, a woman's love is genuine
Things may get rough sometimes
But try to make amends

Because she wants to love for real
If you're in danger, she'll be your shield
But she'll always command respect when she sits
To any man that may hear this, don't fear this

Just make sure that you treat your lady right
Or you'll be up all night
'Cause you got your woman to scream & fight

Just say "I love you & no one else above you"
Except the Lord who I live for
But still, a woman's love is immortal
It's something you can't find going through a portal

So, learn to love what you got
Although you'll struggle a lot
It'll all be good 'cause a woman's love never stops

If she wants the keys to your heart
You ought to give it
'Cause it's a woman's world & sometimes men just live in it

Change for Nobody

To all the ladies with a pretty face
Carrying yourself with grace
Don't let anybody change who you are

You're smart, beautiful and sophisticated
Never let anyone try to change it
You have to change for nobody

There's a man that loves you
Like the Word of God, this is true

Keep walking with confidence
Ignore the nonsense
God's on your side always and every day

You're perfect the way you are
Let no one tell you otherwise
When you look in the mirror, you should say "I'm fine"

Change for nobody

Ignorance Ain't Bliss

Whoever said ignorance is bliss may have lied
At the very least, they were confused inside
They say if you know nothing, don't worry
Even if your perception is blurry

Nowadays, ignorance is no longer bliss
If you don't have enough knowledge, get some quick
We can't go on ignoring the world
Allowing more confusion to unfurl

So, we need to gain some knowledge
Not just some gossip
If it isn't beneficial to anyone
We should just toss it

Ignorance is no longer blissful
Thinking you're better off walking blind is wishful
We need to pull our heads from our rear ends
The more ignorance in the world will cause sheer dread

Be not ignorant & study your lessons
Figure out how to make meaningful impressions
Be not ignorant or you'll be lost
Learning that ignorance has a cost

The cost of ignorance can be your sanity
The cost of ignorance can be your humanity
So, don't let ignorance consume you
Ignorance will only doom you

Don't be ignorant
Be smart
Don't let ignorance make you cold
Keep a good heart

This Little World

This little world we're living in is so swept up in sin
They don't realize what they're doing to themselves
Caught up in increasing their wealth
That they've strayed from the Lord

Little children keep killing each other
Not enough people are reaching each other
Reminding us that we should love one another

Just like God said in the Bible
But instead, we're busy worshipping false idols
Sometimes it's the Benjamins
Other times, it's our famous friends

We must admit that we've fallen from the Lord's Word
Whether it's in the ghetto or the suburbs
It's absurd when you really think about it
The only question is "What could we do about it?"

We could go to the world without an attitude
Repent for our sins & say we want to serve you
Because you're the one & only
Anyone or anything that tried to fill your space is just phony

This little world that we live in is yours & yours alone
Send this message to each & every home
All around the world to every boy & girl
Teach them to strive for more than diamonds and pearls

Every grown man & woman needs to understand
You are the Savior & Creator of Man
You have this little world in your hand
Everything is working according to your plans

This especially must be heard in America
We're lost the most
We need You to bring us close
We need a word from the Holy Ghost

They want to make their own rules & take You out of schools
Everyone wants nothing to do with Your Good News
So, this is evidence that we need to change our ways
Before He comes again in our last days

The Simple Things

Beholding the chance to be holding hands
Being able to share a dance
Giving a kind word to a friend
After arguing, being able to make amends

Being able to see
Being able to breathe
Being able to put your feet on the ground
Being able to walk around

Sharing a hug & sharing some love
Seeing a new day to give praise to the Lord above
Sipping a drink & eating a meal
The simple things can feel so real

Cherish them

Having shoes on your feet
Having an air conditioner to avoid the heat
Putting on a coat amidst the winter cold
Having a wrinkle when you begin to grow old

Be grateful for the simple things
Some may never get the things we take for granted
Don't stay upset when things go wrong
Be grateful that you are still going strong

You could be the one that's out sleeping in the cold
You could be the one who never grows old
You could be the one who is unable to see
You could be the one with no food to eat

You could be the one left wishing for love
Hoping someone will give you a hug
You could be the one with no shoes on your feet
No air conditioner to keep you cool in the heat

You could be the one without a friend
Be grateful for the simple things that makes us men

-Able

I can beat the unbeatable
Touch the untouchable
Move the unmovable
Break through obstacles people say are unbreakable
Keeping my faith strong because I am unshakeable
I can do all things that you think are inconceivable
Reach for goals some people say are unreachable
Come up with plots some would say are unthinkable
Share thoughts some people feel should be unspeakable

Like share true knowledge to all
So that the life you live can one day be teachable
Bring peace & love to this world
With its turns & twirls, real people see that I am lovable
I can put my feet up & recline at my friend's
house on my friend's couch
The reason is they make me feel comfortable
I try to be a nice guy for real
Not perform an act to keep bad deeds
concealed like Cliff Huxtable

My appetite for a positive life is insatiable
Let me list the goods that I bring to the table...

I believe in God
I believe in love
I believe in treating real people with respect
Despite physical appearances, we are
all the same race – human
I don't speak my soul to scare y'all
But, sometimes I have to speak my soul to bare all like a nudist
So, don't be scared to talk to me
I am very approachable
Maybe I can say something in my rhymes that is quotable
To carry with you through life taking some more strides
So, to explain what I'm about, let me say one more time...

I can beat the unbeatable
Touch the untouchable
Move the unmovable
Break through obstacles people say are unbreakable
Keeping my faith in God is strong and unshakeable
I can do anything you may think is inconceivable
Reach for goals some people say are unreachable
Accomplish fetes you may think are unthinkable
Because I have a strong foundation & my ship is unsinkable

I can bring a lot to the table
I am not telling fables
The message that I am trying to convey is that...
I am able

PART 6

IN THE END . . .

I'm Still You

---※---

I am a man who's optimistic
That any dream I have I can live it
Any goal I have, I can achieve it
God gives me the faith to believe it

That I can make a difference in this world
Shine God's light every boy and girl
But the road will never be easy
Still God always stands near me

Someone out there knows how I feel
Everything I'm saying is so real
Someone may be asking "How can I live my dreams?"
Success today isn't always what it seems to be

And I say that I feel the same way you do
Because I'm still you

When I Go . . .

When I go to meet my Lord above
This is for those special ones that I love
If I leave this Earth before you
I want to leave this message for you

If I never see you again
I'm so happy that I called you a friend
If I get reborn, I'd want to live this life all over again

Remember me with fond memories
Say that I tried to love tenderly
Remember please...

Live in Freedom Everyday
Live in Faith Everyday
Loving is Forever Eternal
Know that deep down, I love you

When I Get to Heaven

When I get to Heaven
St. Peter's gates I'm stepping in
What I'll do or who I'll see, I'm imagining
I may come face to face with Martin Luther King
We'll get to sit down & discuss his dreams

Then by any means necessary, I'll meet Malcolm X
Talk about how Afro-Americans can still progress
Pass all of life's stress with less stress
After that, I think about who I'll meet next

I may walk around & say hi to Lady Di
No paparazzi cameras flashing in her eyes
Discuss philosophy with Gandhi
Knowing that you don't have to tote
an AK if you want to be free

While I'm walking down the streets of gold
Lo & behold I see Marilyn Monroe
Looking as sexy as ever
She could still make the weather warm up in December

She asks if I'm going to the concert
I said, "What concert?"
The one in Soul Heaven, you haven't heard?
It's starting in a few minutes, you should go check it out
You'll see a lot of singers that you already know about
So, I decide to check it out
It can't hurt
But I still hope that it lives up to its worth
I arrive at the concert & observe the scene

From wall to wall, I see celebrities glance to center stage
Jimi had his guitar singing *"Purple Haze"*
Then after that came Marvin Gaye
The crowd grooves as *"Let's Get it On"* starts to play

When he walked off, the crowd became patient
Then came the mighty Temptations
Bring with them the sounds of Motown
Then everybody got down when out came James Brown

Getting on the good foot
Had to stop & look
The crowd went so wild that the place shook

Then out walked Ms. Billie Holliday
Calming the crowd down with her sweet serenade
Mahalia came out to sing with Ella
Their two voices together are stellar

Since I'm in Beulah Land
I had to hear the gospel sounds of Walter
Hawkins & James Cleveland
Saw Elvis there with his Blue Suede Shoes
Jam Master Jay on the ones & twos
Holding down the beat in the Heavenly Pavilion
As Aaliyah sang *"One in a Million"*

It did my soul satisfaction
When I finally got to see Michael Jackson
Moonwalking on stage
Performance off the page

But it began to get late, almost time to go
So Tupac, Biggie & Pun came out & kicked their flows
Finally, Prince sang *Purple Rain* for the finale
My childhood dreams becoming a reality

Happiness is endless in the place of eternal bliss
I'll just reminisce when I get to Heaven

About the Author

Patrick Laurence Charles Meade is a teacher, musician, poet, and author. He has a bachelor's degree in childhood education from The City College of New York (2012) and a master's degree in early childhood education from the same college (2024). Patrick is a musician at St. Paul's Progressive Methodist Church in the Bronx, New York. It's a position that he has proudly served in for almost twenty years.

Patrick enjoys listening to gospel music, rap (good rap music), and R&B. He also enjoys writing his own original songs, poems, scripts, and short skits. Preceding this book were *PoEmotions: Poems of Life, Love, Faith and All Emotions* (2017); *PoEmotions Black History: Our Origins, Our Struggles, Our Future* (2018); *Flowers Grow & Butterflies Fly and Other Short Poems for Children* (2019); *PoEmotions: God and Faith* (2020); and *PoEmotions Black History: The Deeper the Roots* (2021).

Patrick was born & raised in the Bronx, New York, where he still lives.